Changing Matter

Karen Larson

Consultant

Michael Patterson
Principal Systems Engineer
Raytheon Company

Image Credits: pp.20–21 (background) Robert Harding World Imagery/Alamy; p.32 ZUMA Press, Inc/Alamy; p.19 (illustrations) Tim Bradley; p.24 Lexa Hoang; pp.2–5 (background), 7 (right), 8–10, 11 (bottom right), 12–13 (background), 13 (bottom & right); 14–15 (background), 16–17, 22–23, 25, 30–31 iStock; p.25 (top) Jessica Gow/epa/Newscom; pp.28–29 (illustrations) J.J. Rudisill; p.25 (bottom) Pascal Goetgheluck/Science Source; all other images from Shutterstock.

Library of Congress Cataloging-in-Publication Data

Larson, Karen, 1951- author.
  Changing matter / Karen Larson.
    pages cm
  Summary: "We all know the three states of matter: solid, liquid, and gas. But what defines these different states? And what's plasma? What if something is in between states? Is a solquid a real thing? Perhaps there's more to matter than simply being a solid, a liquid, or a gas!"—Provided by publisher.
  Audience: K to grade 3.
  Includes index.
  ISBN 978-1-4807-4642-8 (pbk.)
  ISBN 978-1-4807-5086-9 (ebook)
  1. Matter—Properties—Juvenile literature.
  2. Change of state (Physics)—uvenile literature. I. Title.
  QC173.16.L37 2015
  530.4'74—dc23
                                    2014034264

Teacher Created Materials

5301 Oceanus Drive
Huntington Beach, CA 92649-1030
http://www.tcmpub.com
ISBN 978-1-4807-4642-8
© 2015 Teacher Created Materials, Inc.
Printed in China

Table of Contents

What Is Matter?

When people ask, "What's the matter?" they're asking how you feel. But when people ask, "What is matter?" they're not asking about your feelings. They're asking you a science question!

Look at the world around you. Everything you see is matter. The clouds in the sky are matter. The ball hidden under your bed is matter. The crunchy, red apple in your lunch is matter, too. So is the apple juice in your cup! Matter is large, and matter is small. It comes in many forms. The Golden Gate Bridge, a soccer ball, and even YOU are all examples of matter.

Golden Gate Bridge

Properties of Matter

Matter comes in many forms. And it has different **properties** depending on its form. A property is a quality that an object has. It is something about an object that you can see, measure, or hear. It is something you can observe. The color of something is a property. Red is a property of an apple. Size is a property, too. Extreme height is a property of a skyscraper. Even taste can be a property. Sweetness is a property of sugar. Knowing the properties of an object helps us better understand it.

More About Mass

Mass is not the same as weight. Mass always stays the same—wherever you are. Gravity is the force that pulls us and everything else on the planet toward Earth. So something will weigh more on Earth (where there is more gravity) than it does on the moon (where there is less gravity).

Space and mass are two properties that are found in all matter. All objects take up space. A computer takes up space on a desk. You take up space in your chair. A drink takes up space in a glass. Even air takes up space in a balloon!

All objects also have mass. Mass is the amount of "stuff" in an object.

States of Matter

Matter can take the form of a solid, a liquid, or a gas. Each state of matter has its own unique properties.

Solids

Solids can be hard or soft. They can be big or small. Wood is solid matter. Plastic, metal, stone, bone, straw, sand, and crackers are all solids. Man-made solids include everything from computers to keys to the clothes you wear. Ice is a familiar solid. It is the solid state of water. Objects in a solid state don't change shape easily.

Inside Matter

Matter is made up of **molecules**. These particles are too small to see with the human eye. Molecules may be very small, but they are also very important. Their speed determines the state matter takes.

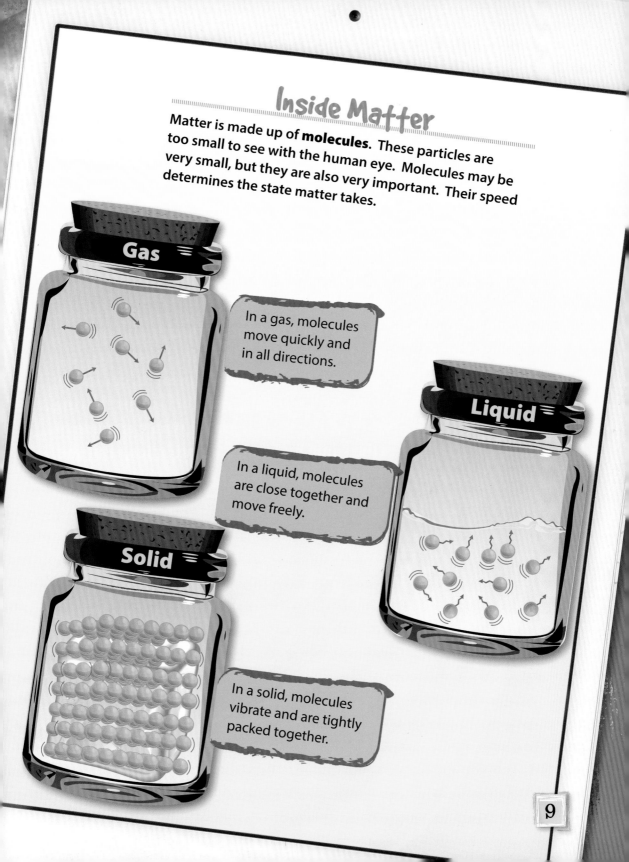

Gas

In a gas, molecules move quickly and in all directions.

Liquid

In a liquid, molecules are close together and move freely.

Solid

In a solid, molecules vibrate and are tightly packed together.

Liquids

Unlike solids, liquids do change shape. They can flow, pour, and even be spilled. They change their shape to fill the space around them. Milk, oil, and ink are all liquids. Have you ever accidently knocked over a cup of juice? Most likely, it came flowing out of the cup and spilled all over the place. It may have run off the table and onto the floor. This is because liquid flows freely.

Water is the most common liquid found on Earth. It doesn't have a definite shape, like ice has. Instead, it takes the shape of its container. If there isn't a container, water keeps flowing, just like the spilled juice. Water is made of the same molecules found in ice. But the molecules in water move more freely.

Volume measures how much space matter takes up. The volume of a liquid is often measured with a graduated cylinder or a beaker.

graduated cylinders

250
230
210
190
170
150
130
110
90
70
50
30
10

A Slow Flow

Some liquids flow more slowly than others. Honey flows more slowly than water. Rubber cement is even thicker and flows even more slowly. But it is still a liquid.

Gases

Gases don't have any shape or size of their own. They spread quickly to fill the space around them. Similar to liquids, gases flow easily. But they can also be **compressed**, or squeezed. One example of compression is a basketball. Gas is forced into a small hole on the ball with an inflator needle. When the needle is removed, the hole closes. Gas can only escape if the hole opens.

Hot air balloons use heated gas to carry people though the air.

Gases are often invisible. So most of the time, we cannot see them. But gases are all around you. Even an empty glass is filled with air. The air we breathe in is a mixture of multiple gases. One of the gases is oxygen.

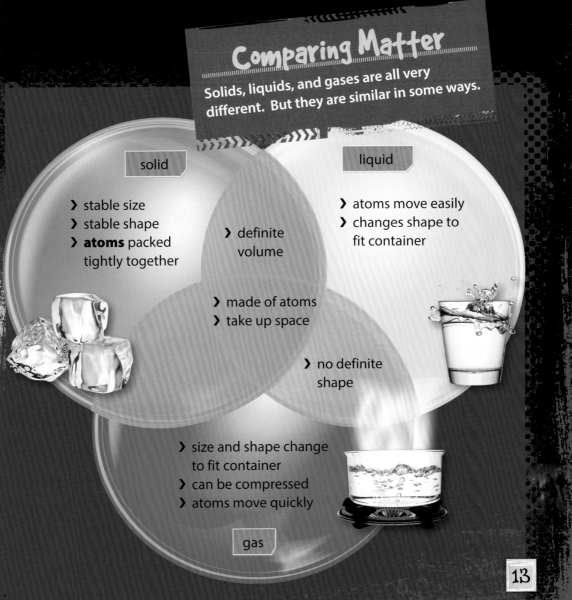

Comparing Matter

Solids, liquids, and gases are all very different. But they are similar in some ways.

solid
> stable size
> stable shape
> **atoms** packed tightly together

> definite volume

> made of atoms
> take up space

> no definite shape

liquid
> atoms move easily
> changes shape to fit container

> size and shape change to fit container
> can be compressed
> atoms move quickly

gas

Many people think there are only three states of matter. But there are actually more! Plasma is the fourth state of matter. It is similar to a gas but is affected by **magnets**. And it is often very hot. It's actually the most common type of matter in the universe! It's possible that the universe was formed from a ball of plasma. Today, plasma is found in our sun, stars, lightning, and even some TV screens. Scientists are always experimenting to find different ways to use plasma. In the future, plasma may be used to create electrical power.

Plasmas are hard to miss— they glow!

Plasma from the sun is attracted to the north and south poles of Earth. The plasma glows and swirls creating the Aurora Borealis.

The Aurora Borealis

The aurora borealis is a beautiful light show in Earth's northern night sky. It occurs when solar wind moves particles from the sun's atmosphere to Earth's atmosphere. Solar wind is a stream of fast-moving electrons and protons made of plasma.

What About YOU?

Your body is made up of three states of matter. You have solid bones and teeth. Your skin, heart, and brain are also solids. Blood, sweat, and tears are liquids. There is air in your lungs, the area surrounding your brain, and inside your stomach.

solid

gas

But why is blood liquid? Blood must be able to flow freely through your body. Why are teeth solid? They must be strong to grind food so it can be digested. Each part of your body is in a certain state for a certain reason.

liquid

Changing Matter

Matter doesn't always stay the same. There are many ways it can change.

One type of change is a **physical change**. Physical changes occur when the size or state of matter changes. The matter will look and feel different, but it is still made up of the same combination of molecules. It still has the same mass. For example, when butter melts, it changes from a solid to a liquid. But don't let its appearance fool you! It's still butter. It still tastes like butter. It still smells like butter. You can also cool it to turn it back into a solid. Then, you can heat it and turn it back into a liquid. The changes can be reversed and do not last.

Melting butter is an example of a physical change.

Crushing a can changes its size. But its state of matter does not change.

Another kind of change is a **chemical change**. This change occurs when molecules move into different combinations. These changes cannot be undone—it is **permanent** when a new substance is formed. When a wood log is burned, it turns to ash. A chemical change occurs as the log burns. The change cannot be undone. The ashes cannot be cooled to make a log again. The ashes smell and look different from the wood log. The molecules have changed, and something new has been made.

urp

Bodily Changes

Both physical and chemical changes can occur when you eat. Your body might grow in size. And you might experience some unpleasant chemical changes!

Physical Changes:
size, shape, texture, mass, weight

Chemical Changes:
color, sound, smell, flashes of light

19

Heating Matter

Heating matter is one way to change it. After a storm, the ground is soaked with puddles of water. Soon, the sun comes out from behind the clouds. It heats the water on the ground, and the water dries up. It may seem like the water has disappeared. The ground is no longer wet and muddy. But the water didn't really disappear. It just changed states. The liquid rain turns into a gas, and the gas spreads out into the air. When the temperature rises, molecules get excited and move around a lot. As they move more and more, they bounce off one another. If enough heat is added, the substance changes states.

Heat can also melt a solid into a liquid. Imagine a solid ice cube sitting in the sun. In time, the sun melts the ice cube into water. Now, the matter is a liquid.

Evaporation

When a liquid is heated and turns to gas, it **evaporates** into the air. Sweating is the body's way of releasing heat into the air. When sweat evaporates, it cools the skin.

Water will evaporate at any temperature as long as the humidity in the air is less than 100 percent.

Cooling Matter

When it gets cold enough, matter can change from a liquid to a solid. Water usually freezes at 0° Celsius (32° Fahrenheit). That is why ice cubes can be found in your freezer. Ice can also be found outside during winter. And ice can be found all year at the North Pole!

Changing Your Mind

Temperature changes can be reversed. Try freezing juice into an ice pop. That's one phase change. But you can create a second phase change easily—just stick the ice pop in your mouth! The heat inside your mouth melts the solid ice pop back into a liquid.

TEMPERATURE

HIGH

LOW

GAS

LIQUID

SOLID

Condensation

The opposite of evaporation is condensation. Condensation occurs when a gas changes to a liquid. Take a look at this glass of soda.

When water vapor bumps into the glass, it turns into water droplets (liquid).

Matter can also change from a gas to a liquid when it is cooled. In the morning, you may see water on the grass and wonder how it got there. During the day, water vapor rises into the air. But at night, the air becomes cooler. The water vapor turns back into drops of water. These small water drops are known as *dew*. This happens because, just like when molecules speed up as they are heated, they slow down as they are cooled. If the molecules slow down enough, the water droplets will change states again.

Squeezing Matter

   Squeeze your hand into a fist. That tight feeling is pressure. Pressure can also change matter from one state to another. For example, solids deep inside Earth can be changed to liquid magma with the right amount of pressure and heat.

Phase Diagram

A phase diagram is a simple way to see the state of matter that things will be in at different temperatures and pressures.

high

Pressure

solid

liquid

gas

low

Temperature

Pressure and heat change rock to magma deep underground. After magma bursts through a volcano, it is called *lava*.

Why Matter Matters

Without matter, there would be no you. Without matter, there would be no universe. Matter is the "stuff" that all things are made of. It can change form. But each state of matter has its own unique properties. We can't pass through solids unless we cut or break them. That's why it's impossible to walk through walls! Liquids change their shape very easily. That's why we don't wear scarves made of hot chocolate! Gases spread out through the air. That's why sitting in a gas chair wouldn't work!

Matter is all around us. It's even in us. Understanding the different states of matter helps us better understand the world we live in. And that matters!

Water is the only substance that occurs in nature as a solid, a liquid, and a gas.

Think Like a Scientist

How do you know gas is present if you can't see it? Experiment and find out!

What to Get

- antacid tablet, such as Alka-Seltzer®
- balloon
- plastic bottle
- water

What to Do

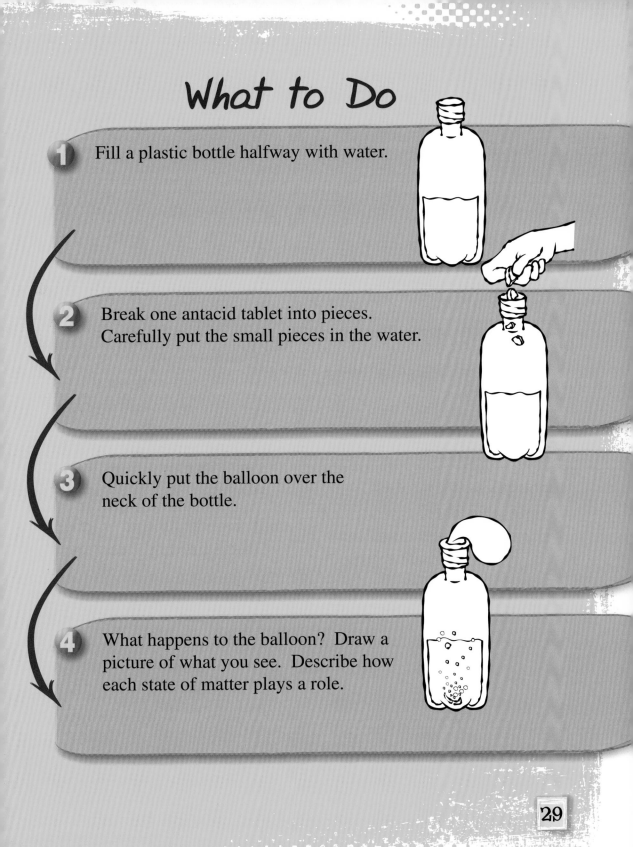

1 Fill a plastic bottle halfway with water.

2 Break one antacid tablet into pieces. Carefully put the small pieces in the water.

3 Quickly put the balloon over the neck of the bottle.

4 What happens to the balloon? Draw a picture of what you see. Describe how each state of matter plays a role.

Glossary

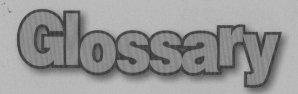

atoms—tiny particles that make up all matter

chemical change—a change that results in new substances

compressed—pressed together

evaporates—changes from a liquid into a gas

magnets—materials that attract certain metals

molecules—the smallest possible amounts of a particular substance that have all the characteristics of the substance

permanent—lasting for a very long time or forever

physical change—a change that does not form a new substance

pressure—the weight or force that is produced when something presses or pushes against something else

properties—special qualities or characteristics of something

volume—the amount of space that is filled by something

Index

Your Turn!

Gloop Soup

Mix corn starch and water together in a bowl. Add more water to make it thinner. It will flow like a liquid. Add more corn starch to make it thicker. It will become harder, like a solid. Squish the gloop between your fingers. Drip it into the bowl. Is it a solid or a liquid? How do you know?